TANI ADAMS

iUniverse books may be ordered through booksellers or by contacting:

iUniverse
1663 Liberty Drive
Bloomington, IN 47403
www.iuniverse.com
844-349-9409

Because of the dynamic nature of the Internet, any web addresses or links contained in this book may have changed since publication and may no longer be valid. The views expressed in this work are solely those of the author and do not necessarily reflect the views of the publisher, and the publisher hereby disclaims any responsibility for them.

Any people depicted in stock imagery provided by Getty Images are models, and such images are being used for illustrative purposes only. Certain stock imagery © Getty Images.

ISBN: 978-1-6632-1716-5 (sc)
978-1-6632-1717-2 (e)
978-1-6632-1795-0 (hc)

Library of Congress Control Number: 2021901400

Print information available on the last page.

iUniverse rev. date: 01/30/2021

ZEN LLAMA ZEN by Tani Adams

© 2019 Tani Adams

Tani Adams

This book is dedicated to anybody who has ever had a bad day and needs to find their happy place; Especially when your happy place is with Llamas and Alpacas. I also want to give thanks to all my family who believed in me and encouraged me to follow my dreams.

ZEN LLAMA ZEN

"When you are having a bad day;
Feeling like you just can't win!
Take a deep breath; Count to ten...

Keep this book near; keep your mind clear...
Thinking positive thoughts will make the
negative disappear.

Llamas doing Yoga may be a place to start,
Bringing joy and happiness when your day
seems torn apart.

Take in deep breath then blow it all out,
Staying calm and relaxing is what this book is
all about.
Start with one, counting upward with these
silly yoga llamas will bring joy within.

Your mind will be clear, and the day will shine
bright once again."

"Llamaste"

"Find you something are Passionate About Keep and tremendously interested in it." Julia Childs

"Imagine

With all your mind.

Believe

With all your heart.

Achieve

With all your might."

AUTHOR UNKNOWN

#6

Nobody is PeRfecT! that's why PENCILS have ERASERS!"

Wolfgang Riebe

"You are Smart
You are
Creative
You are an
Inspiration to
others"

Tani Adams

5

FIVE

You are
Super Duper
Amazing
Talented
Go Getter
Let Nothing
Ever Get in
Your Way

Tani Adams

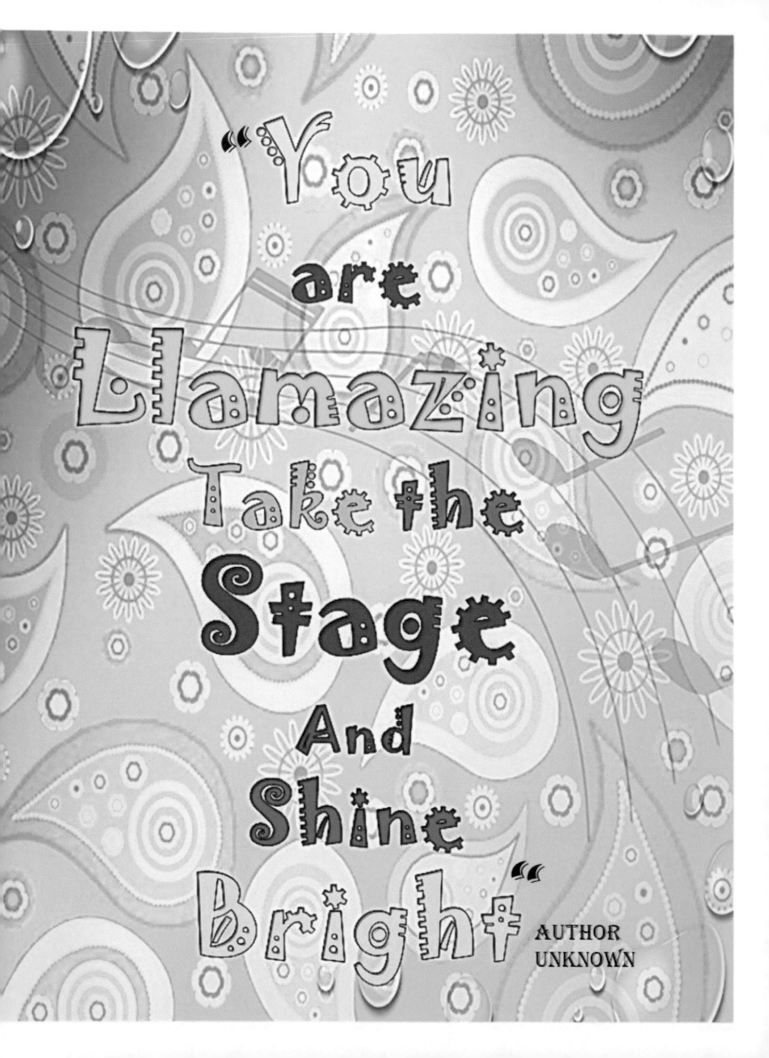

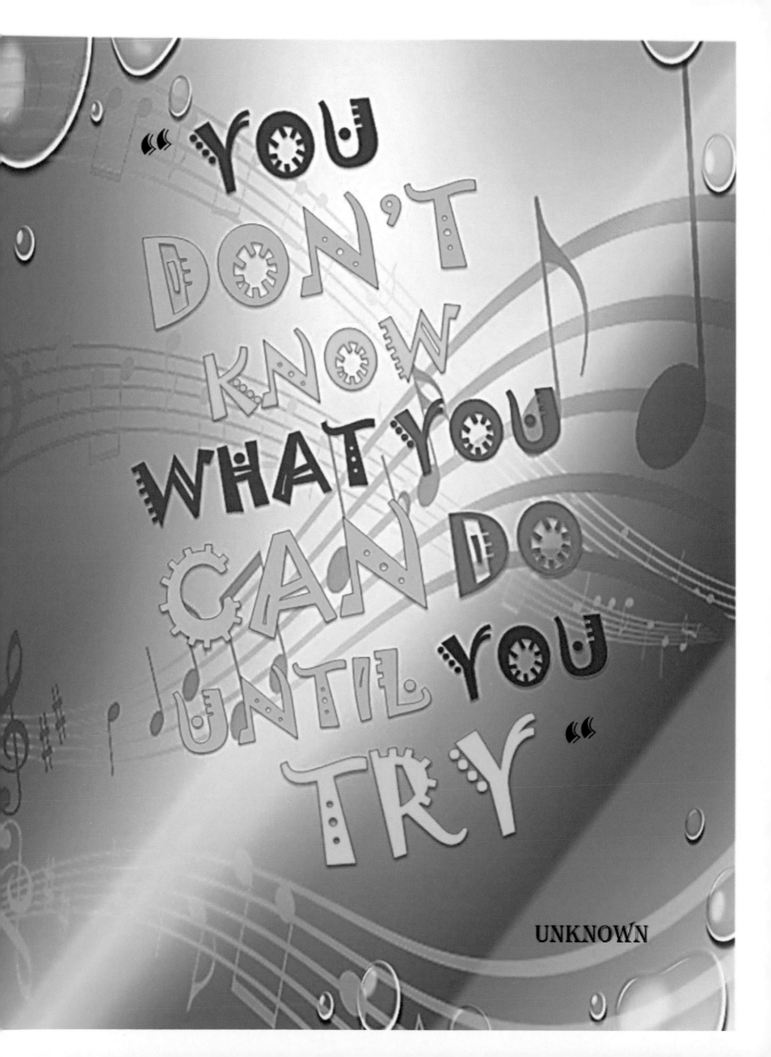

"You can do anything you put your mind to!"

UNKNOWN

"Kindness is FREE SHAREsome Wherever YoU may BE"

SELF RELIANCE

"SomE Days You GoTTa CReaTe YouR OwN SuNShiNe"

SELF RELIANCE

ZEN LLAMA ZEN

THAT WAS FUN

LET'S DO IT

AGAIN

MAYBE NEXT

TIME WITH

FRIEND

Printed in the United States
By Bookmasters